Beneath the Sun

Written by

Melissa Stewart

Illustrated by

Constance R. Bergum

PEACHTREE
ATLANTA

For Dottie, who has filled my world with sunshine
since the day I was born
—*M. S.*

To Ron, my husband and dearest friend
—*C. R. B.*

Published by
PEACHTREE PUBLISHERS
1700 Chattahoochee Avenue
Atlanta, Georgia 30318-2112
www.peachtree-online.com

Book design by Constance R. Bergum and Loraine M. Joyner

Illustrations created in watercolor on 100% rag acid-free archival watercolor paper.
Title typeset in ITC Britannic Bold; text typeset in ITC Veljovic.

Printed in October 2016 by Tienwah Press in Malaysia
10 9 8 7 6 5 4 3 2

Library of Congress Cataloging-in-Publication Data
Stewart, Melissa, author.
 Beneath the sun / by Melissa Stewart ; illustrated by Constance Bergum.
  pages cm
 Audience: 2-6.
 Audience: K to grade 3.
 ISBN: 978-1-56145-733-5
 1. Animal behavior—Juvenile literature. 2. Animals–Adaptation–Juvenile literature.
 3. Sun—Juvenile literature. I. Bergum, Constance Rummel, illustrator. II. Title.
 QL751.5.S74 2014
 591.5—dc23
                                 2013026214

On the hottest days of the year, the sun rises early. Its bright light shines down on us, hour after hour.

You put on sunscreen and spend your afternoons zigzagging under a sprinkler and sipping lemonade.

But many animals struggle to survive beneath the burning sun.

*Beneath the sun
in a field...*

...a woodchuck
munches on grass
in the early morning
light. As the day heats
up, it takes cover in a
cool underground den.

An earthworm stops tunneling through the soil and loops its long, lean body in a tight ball. Its five hearts beat more slowly as it waits for cooler days.

A spittlebug squirts milky white goo out of its abdomen and whips it into a bubbly froth. Inside its foamy home, the little insect stays safe from enemies and the sun's sizzling rays.

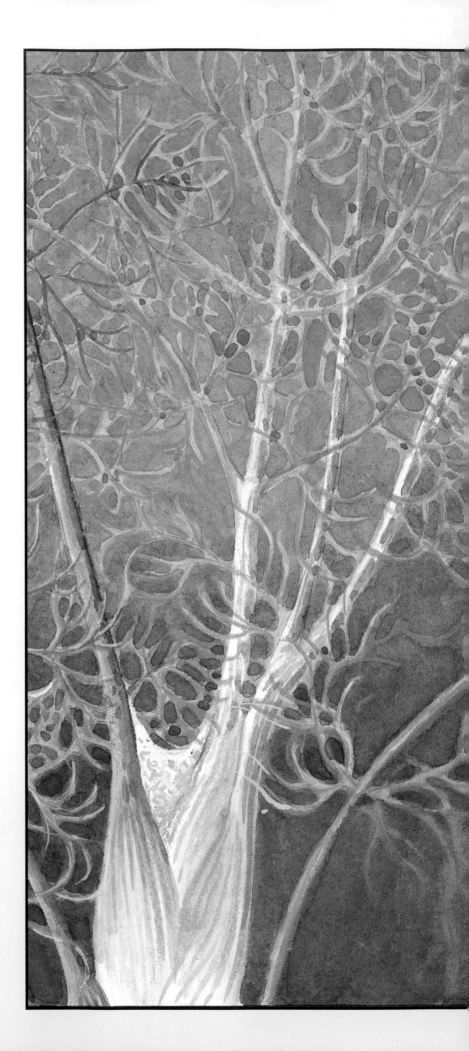

A black swallowtail caterpillar doesn't mind the heat. It keeps chewing and chomping all day long.

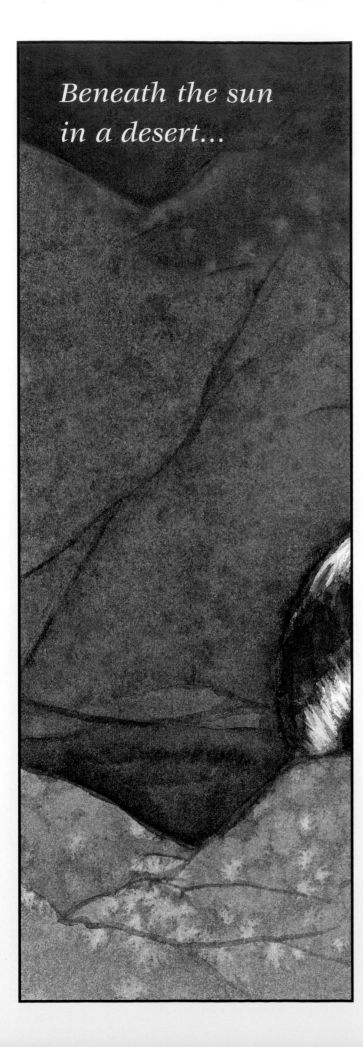

Beneath the sun in a desert...

...a ringtail family sleeps the day away inside a cool, rocky den.

A golden eagle soars through the cool air high above the desert. Its thick feathers shield its skin from the sun's hot rays.

A turkey vulture cools down by spraying urine on its legs.

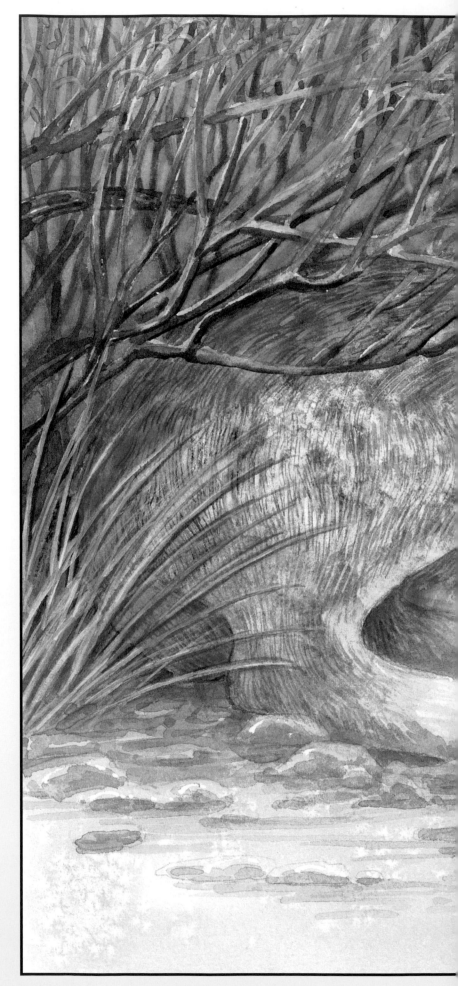

A jackrabbit hides in the shadows. Its body loses
heat through the thin skin on its oversized ears.

A horned lizard stretches out in the shade of a shrub, making its body almost invisible. If an enemy gets too close, the lizard puffs up its body and squirts blood out of the corners of its eyes.

Beneath the sun
in a wetland...

...a male osprey soaks his belly feathers in the water to cool off. When he returns to his nest, three thirsty chicks suck his feathers dry.

Tadpoles grow quickly in the warm wetland water.

They sprout legs,

lose their tails,

and turn into frogs.

Crayfish and siren salamanders can't take the heat. They burrow into the mud to stay moist and cool.

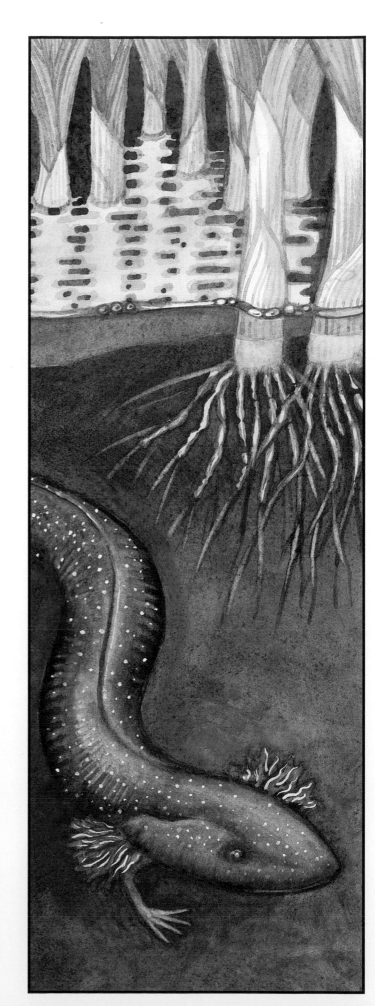

*Beneath the sun
on a seashore…*

…a herring gull shades
its chicks from the sun's
scorching rays. The bird
pants like a dog so it
won't overheat.

Sea anemones pull
in their tentacles
and sit tight.

Sea stars hide in the shade
of a dense seaweed mat.

Fiddler crabs scuttle across the sand. While sunlight streams down, their shells lighten to reflect the sun's bright light.

As the sun slowly
sinks, shadows spread
across the land.

Bands of crimson clouds
set the sky aglow.

Animals living in fields
and deserts, wetlands
and seashores know
that the cool, dark night
is coming.

And so do you.